The Civil War

Contents

Slaves had no freedom. Their lives were controlled by the people who owned them. Families could never be sure that they would be able to stay together.

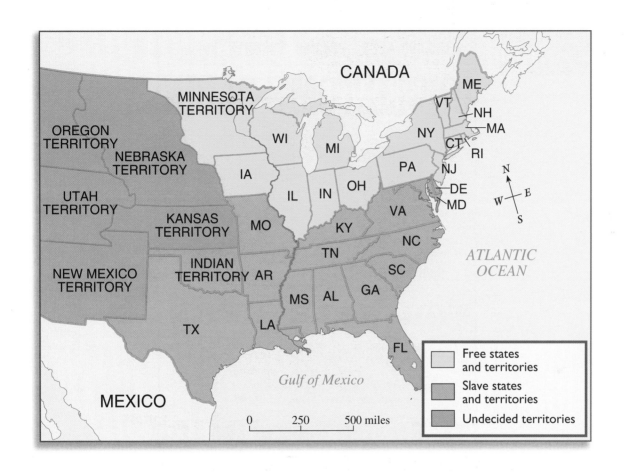

By the 1850s, the United States was divided into slave states and free states. Which way would the territories go—free or slave?

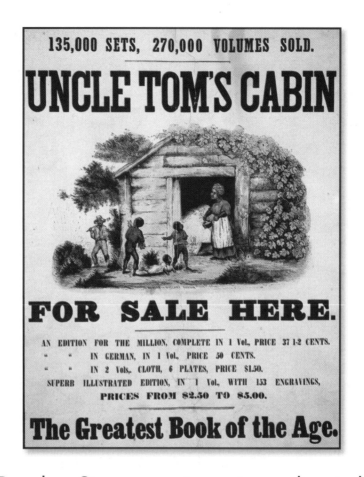

Harriet Beecher Stowe wrote a story about slavery. It was called *Uncle Tom's Cabin.* Many people around the world read it. They learned how bad slavery was.

Harriet Tubman is standing on the left. She
escaped from slavery. Then she went back
many times to help other people escape.
She was a brave person.

This painting shows slaves arriving at a station on the Underground Railroad. Some families in the North helped escaping slaves.

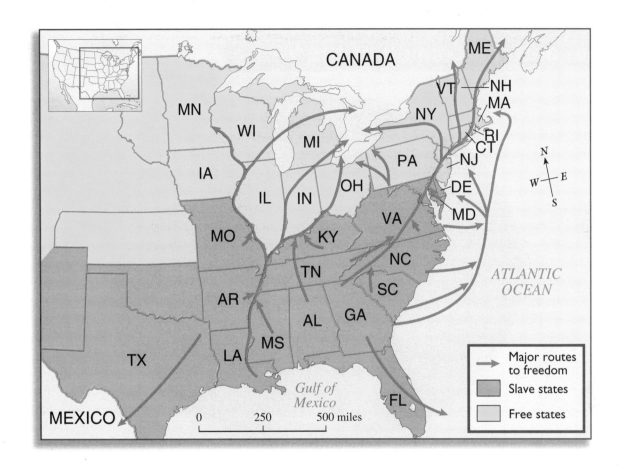

Most of the Underground Railroad routes went north to the free states and to Canada. Some slaves escaped south to places outside of the United States.

Abraham Lincoln was poor growing up.
He had very little schooling. That did not stop
him. Lincoln taught himself to be a lawyer.

In 1860, Lincoln wanted to become President.
He believed the United States should not be
divided into slave states and free states.

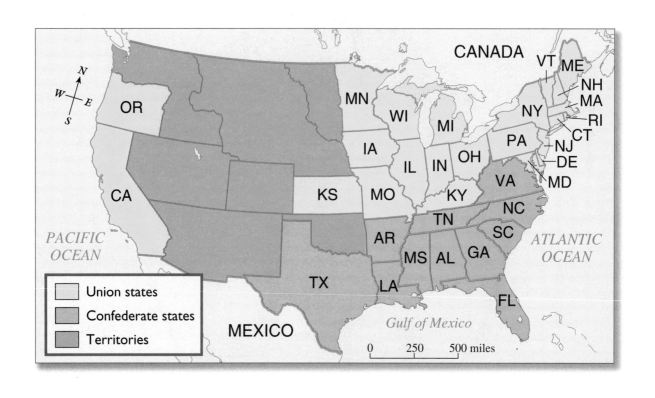

Abraham Lincoln was elected President. Eleven Southern states said they were going to start their own country. How many states stayed in the Union?

Confederate soldiers fired on and captured Fort Sumter in Charleston, South Carolina. President Lincoln said this was an act of war.

War was declared. Both sides prepared for battle. These toy soldiers show what the Confederate and Union uniforms looked like.

The first battle of the Civil War took place
near Washington, D.C. People came to
watch. They were sure that the Union
soldiers would win easily.

President Lincoln's Emancipation Proclamation freed slaves in the South. Many African Americans were grateful to Lincoln.

Robert E. Lee led the Confederate Army.
Ulysses S. Grant led the Union Army. They both
were graduates of West Point Military Academy.
This picture shows how West Point looked.

Robert E. Lee was a very good general. He is shown here on his favorite horse—Traveler. Do you think that is a good name for a soldier's horse?

Ulysses S. Grant also was a very good general.
He did not believe in fancy uniforms. He liked
to be plain and simple.

Richmond, Virginia, was the Confederate
capital. It was in ruins when the war ended.

It was hard for General Lee to surrender his Confederate army to General Grant. When he did, the war was over.

President and Mrs. Lincoln went to watch a play. They were celebrating the end of the war. John Wilkes Booth shot the President.

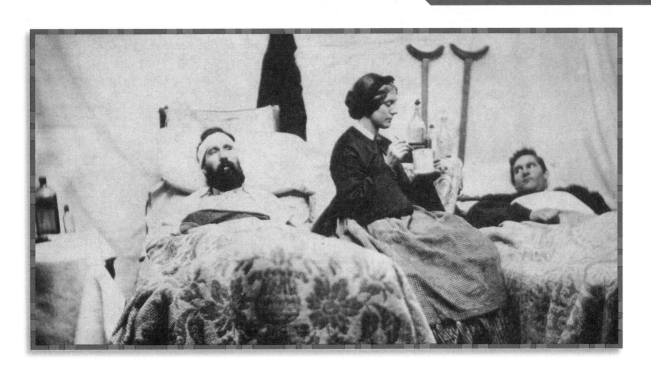

Many women became nurses during the Civil War. They turned their homes into hospitals when battles took place nearby.

Clara Barton was working in Washington, D.C.,
when the war started. She heard that Union
troops needed food and medicine. She loaded
up wagons and drove them to battlefields.

Clara Barton helped wounded soldiers into
trains like this one. They journeyed to hospitals
away from the fighting.

Clara Barton spent the rest of her life helping others. She started the American Red Cross. What do you know about the Red Cross?